Amazing Habitats

TROPICAL RAINFORESTS

W
FRANKLIN WATTS
LONDON•SYDNEY

This edition first published in 2015
by Franklin Watts
338 Euston Road
London NW1 3BH

Franklin Watts Australia
Level 17/207 Kent Street
Sydney, NSW 2000

A CIP catalogue record for this book
is available from the British Library.

ISBN: 978-1-4451-3207-5

Dewey no. 577.3'4

Printed in China

Franklin Watts is a division of
Hachette Children's Books,
an Hachette UK company.
www.hachette.co.uk

Note to parents and teachers concerning
websites: In the book every effort has been
made by the Publishers to ensure that
websites are suitable for children, that they
are of the highest educational value, and that
they contain no inappropriate or offensive
material. However, because of the nature of
the Internet, it is impossible to guarantee that
the contents of these sites will not be altered.
We advise that Internet access is supervised
by a responsible adult.

Author: Leon Gray
Designer: Karen Perry
Picture Researcher: Clare Newman
Editor: Tim Harris
Children's Publisher: Anne O'Daly
Design Manager: Keith Davis
Editorial Director: Lindsey Lowe

Picture Credits
t = top, c = centre, b = bottom, l = left, r = right

The photographs in this book are used by
permission and through the courtesy of:

Front cover: background, ©VWPics/Photoshot; c,
©Vadim Kononenko/Shutterstock.

Inside: 1, ©Kim Briers/Shutterstock; 2-3, ©Szefei/
Shutterstock; 4, ©Gary Tin/Shutterstock; 5t,
©Patrick K. Campbell/Shutterstock; 6cl, ©Wendy
Robert/Dreamstime; 6bl, ©Sorin Vacaru
Photography/Shutterstock; 6bc, ©Dr Morley Read/
Shutterstock; 7t, ©AO Daodaodacod/Shutterstock;
7b, ©Sergey Uryandnikov/Shutterstock; 8,
©Gwoeii/Shutterstock; 9, ©Michael Sewell visual
Pursuit/OSF/Getty Images; 10, ©Dr Morley Read/
Shutterstock; 11t, ©Patryk Kosmider/Shutterstock;
11b, ©Alfredi Maiquez/Shutterstock; 12-13, ©Hugh
Lansdown/Shutterstock; 14, ©A & J Visage/Alamy;
15l, ©Isarescheewin/Shutterstock; 15r, ©Robert
Harding World Imagery; 16, ©Andrew Molinaro/
Shutterstock; 17, ©Dynamic Foto/Shutterstock;
17b, ©Harald Toepfer/Shutterstock; 18, ©Iran
Kuzmin/Shutterstock; 19, ©Martin Harvey/
Photolibrary/Getty Images; 20c, ©Sergey
Uryadnikov/Shutterstock; 20bl, ©Tui De Roy/FLPA;
21t, ©Dr Morley Read/Shutterstock; 21b,
©Heelsky/Shutterstock; 22, ©Front Page/
Shutterstock; 23t, ©Ekk Stock/Shutterstock; 23b,
©Gualtiero Buffi/Shutterstock; 24c, ©Casa da
Photo/Shutterstock; 24-25, ©Mark Hannaford/John
Warburton-Lee Photography/Alamy; 26b, ©Matey
Hudovernik/Shutterstock; 27t, ©Listette Van Der
Hoorn/Shutterstock; 27b, ©Tengku Bahar/Getty
Images; 28cl, ©Patrick K. Campbell/Shutterstock;
28cr, ©Isarescheewin/Shutterstock; 28, ©A & J
Visage/Alamy; 29t, ©Casa da Photo/Shutterstock;
29b, ©Tui De Roy/FLPA.

Brown Bear Books has made every attempt
to contact the copyright holder. If you have
any information please contact
licensing@brownbearbooks.co.uk

CONTENTS

INTRODUCTION

Tropical rainforests grow in warm countries near the **equator**. These dark, rainy **habitats** are home to an amazing variety of animals and plants.

White-lined monkey frogs live on trees in the rainforests of South America.

The places where animals or plants live and grow are called habitats. Some animals and plants live in deserts, grasslands or oceans. And some have **adapted** to survive in rainforests. Warm, wet tropical rainforests are found in many countries of the world, but only grow close to the equator, between the Tropic of Cancer and the Tropic of Capricorn. These two imaginary lines circle our planet north and south of the equator in an area known as the tropics.

Read on to find out what tropical rainforests are like – and how plants, animals and people live in them.

WET WORLD

Heavy downpours flow into rivers and streams that flow through tropical rainforests. This water supports the many animals and plants that live there.

RAINFORESTS OF

Rainforests are found in most tropical areas of the world. The largest rainforests are in South America, central Africa and Southeast Asia.

Dense rainforests cover the tiny Hawaiian island of Oahu in the Pacific Ocean.

NORTH AMERICA

EUROPE

TROPIC OF CANCER

EQUATOR

SOUTH AMERICA

TROPIC OF CAPRICORN

The Arenal Volcano looms large above the Monteverde cloud forest of Costa Rica, Central America.

The River Cononaco snakes through the Amazon rainforest in Ecuador.

ANTARCTICA

THE WORLD

Rainforests

A rainforest in Thailand in Southeast Asia.

AFRICA

ASIA

AUSTRALIA

A photographer on a trip through the rainforests of the Congo River basin, in central Africa.

CLIMATE

Rainforests help to create the rain that gives them their name by playing their part in the **water cycle**. The water cycle is a key reason we have life on Earth.

WATER

In a single year, enough rain falls on the Amazon rainforest to fill 2,000 million olympic-sized swimming pools.

Tropical rainforests are warm because they grow close to the equator, where the Sun's heat is at its strongest. The heat of the tropical sunshine **evaporates** the water on Earth's surface quickly, making the air very **humid**. Imagine sitting in a hot bath. The steam that fills your bathroom is the water that has evaporated. In the rainforest, the steam is the mist and clouds that form as humid air rises above the forest **canopy**. As it rises, the mist cools and gathers together in water droplets. These fall as rain.

Tropical storms

Since rainforests are so warm and the air is so humid, thunderstorms are common. Huge clouds build up above the rainforest canopy as more and more water evaporates into the air. As the warm air rises it cools. The water vapour turns into a liquid and rain pours down onto the forest below.

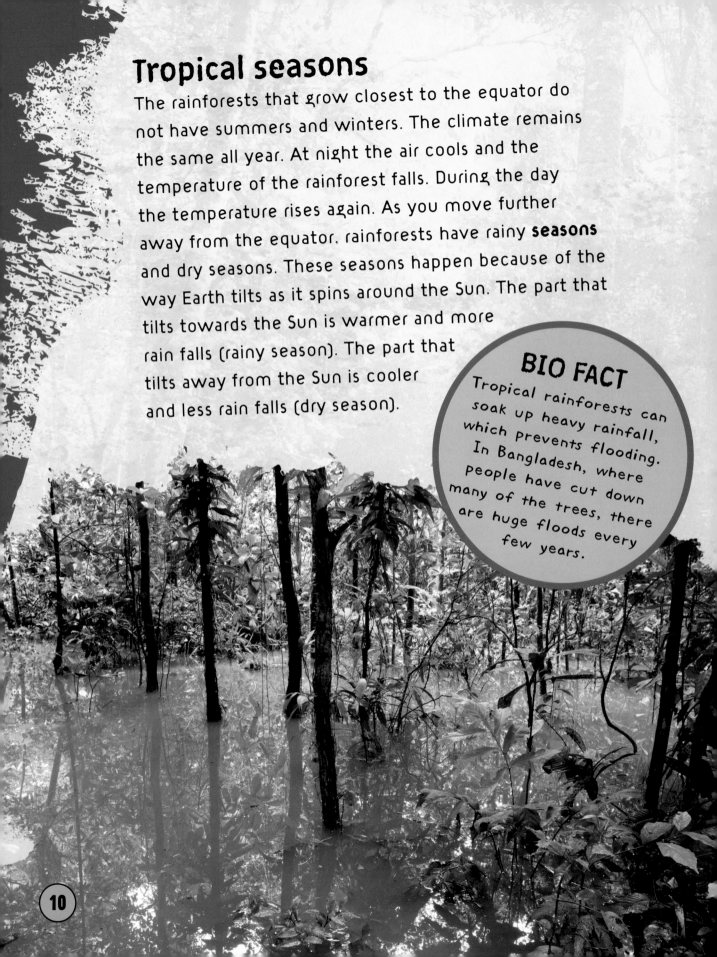

Tropical seasons

The rainforests that grow closest to the equator do not have summers and winters. The climate remains the same all year. At night the air cools and the temperature of the rainforest falls. During the day the temperature rises again. As you move further away from the equator, rainforests have rainy **seasons** and dry seasons. These seasons happen because of the way Earth tilts as it spins around the Sun. The part that tilts towards the Sun is warmer and more rain falls (rainy season). The part that tilts away from the Sun is cooler and less rain falls (dry season).

BIO FACT
Tropical rainforests can soak up heavy rainfall, which prevents flooding. In Bangladesh, where people have cut down many of the trees, there are huge floods every few years.

Tropical island

Tiny patches of rainforest often thrive on islands in the tropics, such as this one in the Maldives in the Indian Ocean. There are no summers or winters here. The warm sea makes the air humid, creating frequent rainfall that encourages plants to grow.

Some rainforest plants, called **epiphytes**, grow on trees and collect the rainwater that drips down the branches.

PLANTS

Tropical rainforests are home to an enormous variety of plant life, from tall trees that poke above the canopy to tiny shrubs that grow on the **forest floor**.

The plants in a rainforest grow in a series of layers. The forest floor at the very bottom is covered with moss and other simple plants, but mainly with rotting leaves and dead flowers. It is damp and dark because the tree canopy blocks out the sunlight.

The layer above the forest floor is called the understory. It is a dense tangle of shrubs, young trees and vines. These plants grow in the shade of taller trees, which make up the rainforest canopy. Many types of epiphyte grow on trees, from the understory to the canopy.

The very tallest trees actually poking through the canopy form the **emergent layer**, which is very sunny during the day because it is above the canopy.

WOW!

● Rainforests are home to some of the tallest trees in the world.

● The Kapok tree grows in the Amazon rainforest, in South America. It can reach up to 70 metres (220 ft) tall.
It's trunk measures more than 4 metres (13 ft) across.

BIG ROOTS
The trees in the emergent layer have wide 'buttress' roots that spread across the forest floor to support the weight of the trees.

Animal attraction

Rainforest plants are usually very colourful. The bright flowers are not just for decoration; they help to attract animals, such as insects and birds. The flowers produce a sugary liquid called **nectar** and dust-like particles called **pollen**. Birds and insects that are attracted to the colourful flowers are rewarded with a drink of nectar. As they drink, pollen sticks to the bodies of these animals. When the birds and insects visit other flowers, the pollen rubs off on the plant. This process is called **pollination**. It means the plants can produce fruits and seeds, which in turn are spread out in the forest and grow into new plants.

Rafflesia plant

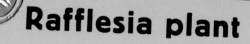

This plant has the largest flower of all plants. It is found only in the rainforests on the islands of Sumatra and Borneo, in Southeast Asia. The giant red and white flower is more than 1 metre (3 ft) wide and stinks of rotting flesh! The smell attracts insects that move pollen from male to female flowers.

FROG FOOD

Beetles and flies live inside the flowers of *Heliconia* plants, which grow in some rainforests. Tree frogs are attracted to these plants because they eat the insects that live there.

Red-eyed tree frog.

Tree frogs crawl over flowers in search of beetles and flies.

Insects hide inside the flowers.

Many rainforest birds, such as the little spiderhunter, feed on the nectar of flowering plants. Spiderhunters also eat spiders.

ANIMALS

The variety of animal life in the tropical rainforests is astounding – there are more **species** than in almost any other habitat on Earth. Scientists are still finding new species.

GORILLAS

Mountain gorillas live in some tropical rainforests in Africa. Young gorillas stay in their family group until they are at least eight years old.

In a South American rainforest, a tree frog waits on a twig until a moth flies past. The frog will catch the moth with its sticky tongue.

Every type of animal can survive in the warm, wet rainforest climate, from insects and birds to reptiles and mammals. Scientists estimate that more than 50 per cent of the world's animal species live in the rainforest. Each animal has adapted to its own way of life. It eats specific food, lives in a specific part of the habitat and uses its own set of skills to stay alive.

Rainforests are home to colourful birds, such as these macaws.

Fruit eaters

Many different animals survive on the abundant supply of fruit in the rainforest. Since there is no summer or winter in the rainforests near the equator, this fruit food is available all year round. Flowering plants produce fruits to help disperse their seeds. When animals such as bats, birds and monkeys eat fruits, the seeds in the fruit are either dropped or pass out of the animals' bodies in their poo. The seeds can then grow into new plants where they land – usually far away from the original plant. The animals therefore help the plants to spread through the rainforest.

BIO FACT

Some fruit bats live in rainforests. They fly around the forest in search of small fruits that grow on trees. The bats suck the juice out of the fruit.

Ape relations

The bonobo is an ape that lives in the dense rainforests of the Congo in Africa. Apes are a group of mammals that includes gorillas, chimpanzees and humans. Like other apes, bonobos live in groups and they are very clever animals. Bonobos feed mainly on the plentiful supply of fruit found in the rainforest but sometimes they hunt other animals for meat.

Rainforest predators

The dense vegetation in rainforests is a perfect hiding place for **predators**, such as birds of **prey**, reptiles and big cats. Owls and eagles swoop between the trees, feeding on small animals; and crocodiles lurk in rivers and streams to snap up animals that stop for a drink. Snakes and tigers lie in wait to ambush passing prey, such as deer and other, smaller mammals.

Nile crocodiles live in rivers that flow through rainforests in Africa. They hunt monkeys, deer, fish and snakes.

Aerial attack

The harpy eagle is one of the deadliest predators of the Central American rainforests. These large birds of prey have enormous, sharp, hooked claws (called talons) on their feet. Their talons can measure up to 13 cm (5 in) long. They use their talons to pluck sloths, lizards and other animals from the treetops.

The Brazilian wandering spider uses its deadly **venom** to kill prey, such as frogs and mice.

BIO FACT
Tigers are top predators that live in the rainforests of South and Southeast Asia.

PEOPLE

From traditional **hunter-gatherers** to the farmers of today, people have been living in harmony with the rainforests for thousands of years. But many others have been exploiting the forests for their rich resources.

MUSIC MEN
People from the village of Kamayura in the Amazon rainforest in Brazil still practise many of their traditions.

Rainforests have been home to people since the very beginning of the human species. The rich variety of plant and animal life has provided people with food, shelter and medicine.

In remote parts of rainforests, a few people still continue to live a traditional way of life. They hunt wild animals, such as birds, deer and monkeys and collect fruits, mushrooms and nuts from the forest. These hunter-gatherers usually live in small groups. Instead of living in houses, some of them build temporary huts for shelter as they move around the forest. This way of life is dying out, however, as other people clear the forests for farming, raising livestock and building permanent homes.

In Southeast Asia people cut the bark of rubber trees to get a white liquid called latex. They make rubber from this.

This traditional long house in Borneo is made from the wood of rainforest trees.

Modern life

Today, most people who live in tropical forest regions have turned to **agriculture** to survive. They have cleared large areas of rainforest to grow crops and raise livestock to feed their families. Rainforests have also been cleared to provide valuable resources, such as coffee, rubber, tea and spices, which the local people harvest and sell. Cities have been built along the rivers that run through prime rainforest habitats. People have built dams across these rivers, harnessing the heavy tropical rains to generate **hydroelectricity**. Unfortunately, the dams also flood the rainforest, killing many of the animals and plants that live there.

In the city

Manaus is the capital city of the Brazilian state of Amazonas. It is built on the banks of the River Negro in the heart of the Amazon rainforest. More than 1.9 million people live in this isolated city.

BIO FACT

Many rainforest plants contain amazing life-saving medicines. Quinine is used to treat malaria. Quinine comes from the bark of the cinchona tree, which grows in the Amazon.

Vast areas of trees in the Amazon rainforest have been felled for agriculture, such as cattle farming.

THE FUTURE

Rainforests around the world are in danger. If these fragile habitats continue to be cleared to satisfy the economic needs of agriculture and industry, many plants and animals will be lost forever.

The future of rainforests is uncertain. A few hundred years ago, these areas of outstanding natural beauty were relatively unspoiled. Today, farmers and loggers have changed the landscape forever. Rainforests are disappearing at an alarming rate. Some people believe they could disappear in less than 100 years if this **deforestation** continues. The effects will be devastating. Earth's climate will become warmer and many rainforest animals and plants may become **extinct**.

Orange ape

The orangutan is one of the most endangered animals on Earth. A close relative of humans, this orange ape lives in rainforests on the islands of Borneo and Sumatra in Southeast Asia.

Logging is big business and one of the biggest threats facing rainforests around the world.

PALM OIL

Farmers growing palm trees for oil in Malaysia have faced criticism for destroying the country's rainforests and driving many animals to extinction.

QUIZ

Try this quiz to test your knowledge of rainforest habitats. The answers are on page 31.

1 White-lined monkey frogs live in the rainforests of which continent?

2 What is the name of the sugary liquid this bird is drinking?

3 On which islands do the giant red flowers of the Rafflesia plant grow?

4

What is the name of this city in the heart of the Amazon rainforest?

Fact File

- Most tropical rainforests grow in countries near the equator.
- The climate in rainforests is warm and rainy.
- Rainforests are home to an amazing variety of life.
- Scientists think that rainforests will disappear in 100 years if deforestation continues at its present rate.

5

This bird of prey lives in the rainforests of Central America. What is it called?

Winners and losers

⬆ Farming, logging and mining provide people in developing countries with jobs and money to feed their families.

⬇ Tigers will become extinct if deforestation continues. One hundred years ago, there were 100,000 tigers in the world's rainforests. Today, there are fewer than 3,200 in the wild.

GLOSSARY

adapted: When a plant or animal has changed to help it cope better in its surroundings.

agriculture: The practice of growing plant crops and raising animals for food, clothing and other products.

canopy: The dense layer of trees and other vegetation that forms the top of a rainforest.

deforestation: The process of clearing trees for agriculture, timber and/or other human industries.

emergent layer: The tallest layer of trees above the rainforest canopy.

epiphytes: Plants that grow on other plants without stealing the other plants' water or nutrients.

equator: An imaginary line that passes around Earth's widest point.

evaporates: To turn from liquid to gas when heated.

extinct: When a plant or animal has died out.

forest floor: The bottom layer of the rainforest.

habitats: The places where plants or animals usually live and grow.

humid: When the air contains a high level of water vapour.

hunter-gatherers: People who collect fruits, berries and nuts and hunt wild animals for food.

hydroelectricity: The electricity generated from the water that flows through dams.

nectar: The sugary liquid found inside the flowers of some plants.

pollen: Tiny dust-like particles made by the male parts of a flower.

pollination: When an animal transfers pollen from one plant to another.

predators: Animals that hunt other animals, called prey, for food.

prey: Animals that are hunted by other animals, called predators.

seasons: Periods during the year that have their own distinct weather. In the tropics there is a wet season and a dry season.

species: A group of animals that look alike. Members of the same species can mate and produce young together.

venom: A poison that some animals make in their bodies to attack prey.

water cycle: The journey that water takes as it moves between land, the air and the oceans.

FURTHER RESOURCES

Books

Calver, Paul and Toby Reynolds. *Visual Explorers: Rainforest.* Franklin Watts (2014).

Harrison, Paul. *Up Close: Rainforest.* Franklin Watts (2011).

Newland, Sonya. *Saving Wildlife: Rainforest Animals.* Franklin Watts (2014).

Rockett, Paul. *The Big Countdown: 30 Million Different Insects in the Rainforest.* Franklin Watts (2014).

Websites

BBC Nature. This website introduces our planet's vital rainforest habitats, from the Congo in Africa to the Amazon in South America. Click on the links to view stunning photos and videos of the plants and animals that live in them.
www.bbc.co.uk/nature/habitats/Tropical_and_subtropical_moist_broadleaf_forests

Mongabay. A great website written for young readers. It asks important questions about rainforests and explains why we should save them.
kids.mongabay.com

National Geographic. Explore the world's rainforest habitats. Includes great photographs and links to related National Geographic pages.
environment.nationalgeographic.com/environment/habitats/rainforest-profile/

World Wide Fund for Nature. Photos, videos, animals and plants that live in the world's forests. Read about some of the conservation plans for rain forests at risk, and find out what you can do to help.
worldwildlife.org/habitats/forests

Answers to the Quiz: 1 South America. **2** Nectar. **3** Borneo and Sumatra. **4** Manaus (in Brazil). **5** Harpy eagle.

INDEX

SAINT BENEDICT CATHOLIC
VOLUNTARY ACADEMY
DUFFIELD ROAD
DERBY
DE22 1JD